Foreword

This book does what it *"says on the tin"* – it introduces basic selling skills.

Anyone starting in sales - or someone experienced who wants to revisit the basics - will find it very valuable.

Eric Pillinger   Director   TACK International

Introduction

Everyone is involved in a selling process everyday of their lives, albeit they are not always conscious of that fact -

Selling -

yourself to prospective in-laws

ideas, new approaches at work

the dog for walkies in the rain

your kids to do their homework instead of playing computer games

Selling is a natural but often an unconscious everyday activity.

In business however the winning of orders is paramount, the sales force being the lifeblood of a company.

Without their sales a company fails.

A highly motivated, disciplined and effective sales team is essential to the success of any organisation.

Without sales a company dies.

Sales people are in the front line; they are the company's commandos and also its ambassadors.

Their standards are those by which your customers judge the organisation. Yet many companies inadequately prepare their sales force for this task.

HOWEVER the selling techniques explained in our book are not just directed at frontline sales people, they are valuable across the whole company particularly in after sales services.

The service engineer and the receptionist probably have more regular interaction with your existing customers than your sales force and can be highly influential in creating a positive impression.

Make sure *ALL* of your people are well prepared in this highly competitive world.

Successful Selling: The Basics

By Barry Thorogood and David Butler

Published by: Team International Publications

Website: www.teaminternationalpublications.co.uk

Websites references

Please note that the Website referred to in this book for access to sales documents and related graphics is www.teaminternationalpublications.co.uk

Barry Thorogood

www.teaminternational.co.uk

David Butler

www.davidbutler.co.uk

To Louise

2

Our aim in compiling this book:

To have you consciously recognise the steps in the selling activity and help you dramatically improve your sales capability and thereby your financial success and that of your Company.

We believe **everyone** in an organisation should understand the basics of selling and the vital importance of creating and building upon a strong durable relationship with your customers.

Harvard Business School states that it is 7 (yes SEVEN) times more costly to gain a new customer than to book incremental business from an existing satisfied customer.

So why would you **NOT** teach everyone in the company to value your customers and gain that business?

Is it worth the effort of teaching everyone about selling techniques and how to strengthen the relationship with the customer?

Is it worth spending JUST ONE HOUR reading this book?

YOU BET IT IS!

Yes - you are right - of course everyone would benefit from having a copy of this book!

Remember

The Sales Process is the same whether you are selling a pencil or a battleship!

The basic differences are in the transaction timescale and the number of noughts on the price.

The stark reality is that once you have learned the Selling Process you can sell anything! That makes you a highly prized individual in the job market as the rewards are linked directly to your sales ability.

The Sales Process outlined in this book enables you to earn high salaries and commission. If you are thinking of changing your career and going into sales, then this book is invaluable!

If you are already in sales then this book will assist you to earn big money and improve your life style.

If you are starting your own business then however good your product or service is, if you do not have sales ability, you will fail!

Success depends upon your professionalism and your disciplined approach to the effective activity required. What are the ingredients necessary to become successful in selling?

Read on!

Chapter 1: Setting SMARTER Objectives

The ability to set clear objectives and to communicate them to others is one of the most important skills that you will ever learn.

Studies at Harvard University showed that only 7% of the students set clear goals on leaving. Twenty years later those 7% had amassed more wealth than the other 93% put together.

"But were they happy?" we hear you ask. Well, yes they were. As well as having oodles of dosh, they also consistently scored higher on other criteria i.e. social integration, happy family life and physical health.

The Native American Indians have a concept called "*Hanta Yo*". It means "The Way" or "The Path".

When you are on your path you are powerful.

When you are off your path you feel weak, unsure, dis-empowered and events do not go well for you.

Spend a few moments reflecting on where you are in your life.

Have you set yourself clear objectives?

Do you know when things are going right?

What is your state of mind when they are?

What are your feelings?

What are your thoughts?

Compare these with how you feel, think and act when things are not going right.

Unless you are centred you cannot make good decisions. Also, unless you are totally aware, not just of events going on around you, but more importantly of the things going on inside you, you cannot make good decisions, either.

SMARTER objectives are even more effective than the SMART objectives that are normally taught.

The "E" and the "R" are what makes the difference between those objectives which are ultimately achieved and those that are not.

The letters stand for:

Specific

Measurable

Achievable

Relevant

Time-related

Ecological

Reward

SMARTER !

Let us consider each segment more closely.

Specific

When you state any objective it must be clear and precise.

"I want to be successful." is not specific enough. A successful what? Business person, piano player, pilot?

The objective should be unambiguous, to others as well as yourself, without the need for elaboration or further explanation.

 This acts as a discipline to ensure clarity of thought.

A useful test for this may be asking yourself, or a colleague - Could someone possibly misinterpret this, and if so, how can I change it so that any misunderstanding would be virtually impossible?

Measurable

How will I, and others, know that the objective has been achieved?   How will you measure it?

 If your object was to be a successful business person how will you measure that success?

Will it be a £1,000,000 in the bank or will you pay cash for a £500,000 house or perhaps you will own one factory and ten retail outlets or a thriving online business?

What will you or others see? New behaviours perhaps, or figures on paper.

What will you say, think and feel about that success?

Achievable

Is this objective really achievable?

Can it be done, and if so within my time scale?

Do I have the resources that I will need, i.e. money, people, skills, knowledge, space, materials and time?

If I not, will I be able to acquire them?

Relevant

Does this particular objective fit with the bigger picture of where I am heading? If it is a team objective the same question applies to the team as well as its individual members.

Some people are extremely efficient at achieving their objectives, only to realise later that in doing so they were striding further along the wrong path.

It is easily possible for an unaware person to achieve every one of their irrelevant objectives and be totally ineffective. Do not let this person be YOU!

Time-Related

Have I set a time scale within which I will be able to achieve the objective?

Is it real or do I really expect it to be achieved later, or much earlier? Have I built in too much or too little slack for contingencies?

Set a sensible date and plan a time-line with all the milestones on the way.

If you do not set clear objectives you are likely to drift to an entirely different place, like flotsam and jetsam.

Ecological

Do I feel sufficiently comfortable with the consequences of achieving this objective to pursue it?

Consider the consequences, both immediate and in the future, for yourself and others? For some objectives 'others' may include your family, your team or the natural environment.

Am I willing to spend that amount of time, money, energy or whatever it may take, to achieve this objective?

Am I considering the wider implications of both the pursuit and achievement of this objective or am I viewing it in isolation?

Even the slightest movement creates a wave - how do I feel about the waves?

How much of your own and others resources would be expended in its achievement?

As a salesperson you will require *entrepreneurial skills* to survive in a highly competitive environment.

One definition of an entrepreneur is someone who views everything around him or her as a *resource*. For example, when you are on a train or an aeroplane talk to the person next to you. They may be a useful resource or a potential customer.

 Many deals arrive out of the blue from the most unexpected sources. NEVER STOP SELLING (but don't overdo it!). Be subtle.

The secret is to let the customer buy, rather than you sell.

We have all sat next to someone who tries to ram their product down our throat and the thought of sitting next to them for several hours on a long journey is a nightmare.

Reward

What will you earn for achievement? How will you reward yourself for your efforts?

What would you really like to do or buy that would be commensurate with the importance for you of the objective?

If you earned big money what would you buy? How would it change your Lifestyle?

Visualise this. It is a powerful motivator!

For far reaching objectives reward yourself at milestones along the way.

Never forget others if the achievement is a result of an overall collective effort.

Chapter 2: FAB: Features, Advantages & Benefits

Having set your SMARTER objectives let us get started on selling your way to success!

The whole art of selling is about identifying the needs of the customer and then being able to demonstrate convincingly how your product or service will satisfy those needs and benefit their business.

Many sales people (particularly in technical and IT) concentrate on *features* rather than *benefits* and therefore get stuck in the technical specifications of the product without illustrating the corresponding benefits that these offer to the customer.

Professional selling skills is a process whereby you probe the customer for their needs and match them to the benefits that your product or service can deliver.

Examples of benefits are:

Greater speed, cheaper cost, greater productivity, improved style, ease of use . . . .

So, you may ask, what is the difference between a feature, an advantage and a benefit?

Feature: A feature of a *product* could be its physical characteristics e.g. large, small, square, round, colour, shape, speed . . . .

Exercise 1:   Pick up a pencil. Study it closely. Then in the table below make a list of all its features.

Let us fill in five features as an example:

	Table 1: Features, Advantages & Benefits of a simple pencil		
	Feature	**Advantages**	**Benefits**
1	Six sided	Will not roll off desk Easy to grip	? ?
2	Wooden	Can be re-sharpened Floats Light weight	? ? ?
3	Bright Yellow	Easily seen	?
4	Integral eraser		
5	Lead core		

Advantage: An advantage improves the situation for your customer.

We have also filled in the first three advantages sections on the table.

The advantage *directly relates* to the feature.

Exercise 2:

Now create a table and fill in all the features and corresponding advantages relating to your pencil. You may be surprised how many there are!

Can you find 15?

Benefit: A benefit is an advantage of the product or service that matches a *previously expressed need* of the customer.

Look at Feature 3 in the table. If your prospective customer is colour blind, the fact that the pencil is easily seen because it is bright yellow is of no benefit and therefore for this prospect, the pencil being brightly coloured is not an advantage. It does not improve the situation for the prospect.

An advantage is not beneficial unless the customer says they need it.

In Table 1 we can only complete the benefit column if the customer expresses the need. People will only buy if your product or service matches their needs.

 Without this your product or service has no benefits. Without any benefits, why would they buy from you?

Later on we will show you how to find out the needs of your customer so that you can *match their needs to your product features* and build a list of all the benefits that are important to your prospective customer.

Note that, even for the same product or service, different customers may have different needs!

You can now see how the features of a product are designed to bring corresponding advantages and possible benefits.

How about the features, advantages and benefits of a service?

Features of a service might be 24/7 availability, same day delivery, nationwide coverage, four hour response time or a qualified engineering force.

Using one of the features, a salesperson could say:

"A feature of our service is that our engineers can support all of your factories in the UK within a four hour response time. The advantages are that you get a **rapid response** to all your facilities, **less downtime** and a corresponding **overall production increase**. Would these be of benefit to you?"

If the customer replies "Yes" or nods in the affirmative then write this benefit down for future reference (see 'Building a Benefit Bank' later on in this chapter).

Using another example the same salesperson could say "Our rapid 24/7 engineer service will **minimise production downtime** thereby **increasing profitability** in your factories. Would that be of value to you?"

The customer could reply: "Not really, I do not run my factories 24/7 and the products you support are not key critical to production, so such a service would be an extravagance."

In this case your feature of 24/7 service could actually be a disadvantage due to the costs involved! As a result you cannot add this to your Benefit Bank.

To keep things simple, only deal with one feature and advantage of your product at a time. You can then tease out the corresponding benefits to add to your Benefit Bank.

Beware!

Some salespeople, in their enthusiasm to tell their prospective customer how wonderful their product or service is, spew out all the features and advantages of their product in one big overwhelming barrage without stopping to question whether any of these features and advantages are of any benefit to the customer.

This is **telling** as opposed to **selling** and it is NOT a successful technique!

Having difficulty?

Here's one we prepared earlier!

Have a look at Table 2 on the next page and you will see a FAB sheet for selling our pencil.

The benefits listed are all potential benefits and only become "real" benefits if the customer needs them.

 Later in the book you will learn how to support these benefits in order to underpin and strengthen the sale (see Chapter 12: Support Statements).

Table 2:

FAB Sheet

Using our pencil again

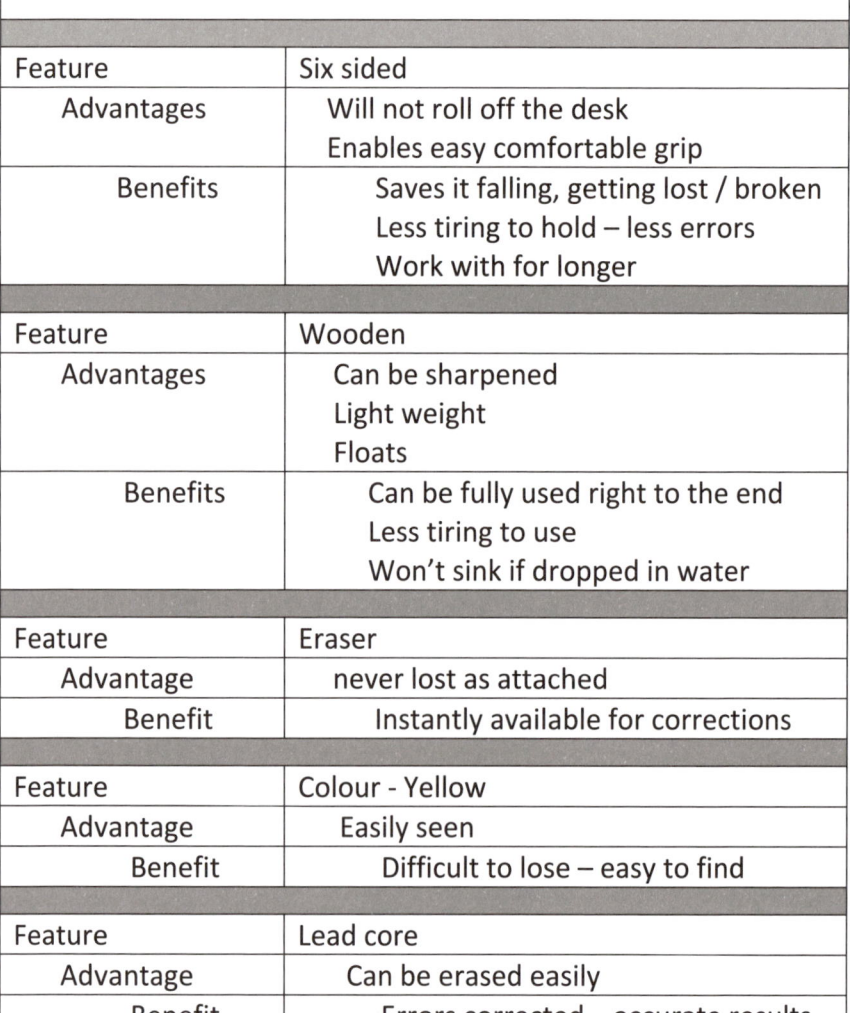

Feature	Six sided
Advantages	Will not roll off the desk
	Enables easy comfortable grip
Benefits	Saves it falling, getting lost / broken
	Less tiring to hold – less errors
	Work with for longer

Feature	Wooden
Advantages	Can be sharpened
	Light weight
	Floats
Benefits	Can be fully used right to the end
	Less tiring to use
	Won't sink if dropped in water

Feature	Eraser
Advantage	never lost as attached
Benefit	Instantly available for corrections

Feature	Colour - Yellow
Advantage	Easily seen
Benefit	Difficult to lose – easy to find

Feature	Lead core
Advantage	Can be erased easily
Benefit	Errors corrected – accurate results

Exercise 3:

Choose an object to try out your understanding of Features, Advantages and Benefits.

List the features on a FAB sheet

Tease out the advantages by asking "so what" for each feature

Now list the corresponding advantages

Make sure that the advantages match the features

Explain for each advantage how the customer will benefit

Remember -

An advantage is not a benefit unless the customer says they need it.

Have a laugh and complete your personal FAB sheet but keep it clean, this is a business book!!!

Exercise 4:

Create your own version of Table 3 and list the features of the product or service that you are currently selling.

Then ask the question *"so what?"*

This is the question that the customer would instinctively ask against each feature and it will prompt you to list the corresponding advantage.

There is a Word version of Table 3 you can download from our website.

Table 3: My Products and Services Description:		
	Feature	Advantages	Benefits
1			
2			
3			

Make certain you thoroughly understand the needs of your customer.

Exercise 5:

Building a Benefit Bank

Use Table 3 to prepare your own table and use it to discuss the features and advantages of your product or service with every potential customer.

If they agree that they have a need then complete the benefit column for each feature.

This is your Benefit Bank.

You can use this later when you come to close the customer for an order. It is called - The Benefit Close.

More about that in Chapter 16: Closing the Sale.

Chapter 3: The Sales Cycle

The Sales Cycle is defined as the time it takes from your first contact with a customer to the time you successfully close an order.

The aim is to make the sales cycle as short as possible. Each product or service has a different sales cycle. Generally the simpler the product or service the shorter the sales cycle, the more complex, the longer the sales cycle.

However this is not necessarily so. Some products are complex e.g. cars, but are connected with self-worth and status. These become emotional decisions and the sales cycle can be very short.

Battleships, power stations or complex computer systems are rational decisions and the sales cycle protracted.

To a sales person the shorter the sales cycle, the quicker you get the order, the quicker you get your commission.

BUT there can be a trade-off here. A longer more complex sale can result in a bigger order. A short quick kill can result in a smaller order and less money.

Ideally you will do what is best for the customer but commission can be alluring. What is your predominant style? What does your commission scheme push you towards?

Could short term-gains hinder a long-term profitable relationship?

People buy from People - your personal integrity and credibility is paramount in that relationship.

One format for defining the sequence within the sales cycle is called SPANCO.

It enables you to tell where you are in the sale and helps you and your manager to forecast income and revenue more accurately.

SPANCO

Suspect,

Prospect,

Analysis,

Negotiation,

Close,

Order

The SPANCO format was designed and used very successfully by the Xerox sales force and in one format or another is a standard tool for sales control by both the sales force and sales management.

Let's look more closely at this essential method of monitoring your progress through the sales cycle:

SUSPECT

This is any business that could use your products or services.

You could compile a list of contacts from Facebook, Linked In, Branch Out, Twitter and similar internet networks. Search local phone books and business directories, walk down the main business streets, visit industrial estates and so on.

These lists of people do not go on the SPANCO records (which could be electronic or paper based), there would simply be too many of them, so we must first qualify each of them by writing, e-mailing, messaging, phoning or calling in to see if they are at all interested in the products or services you are offering.

If they show enough of an interest to make an appointment or want details sent to them, they then become a Prospect and are entered on a record.

PROSPECT

Next you must gauge the extent of the interest. Is it genuine or are they a time waster without a budget?

If this prospect appears genuine enter the value of the product or service that you think you may be able to sell to him, and how long you think the selling cycle will take.

Ask questions like -

> When does the budget become available?
>
> Has your boss given you a deadline to install the system?
>
> When does my rival's existing contract expire?

Finally, estimate from your contact the probability of success from 10% to say 50% - it can only be 100% when the order is signed and this is the early stage.

From these indications you can prioritise your time and concentrate on the most promising prospects.

ANALYSIS

This is the phase when you try to understand the customer's problem in more detail to ensure that your solution really will meet their needs.

If you are trying to sell a computer system you may try to project future data storage requirements locally or in a cloud. If they already have hardware, will it run your software? Do they have skilled staff or will training be required?

After this phase you can update your records to reflect your increasing or decreasing optimism, the change in value of the potential order and be more accurate with the timescale in terms of the order being placed.

NEGOTIATION

Having satisfied yourself and the potential customer that your product can offer significant benefits you are now into negotiation on price, contractual terms and conditions, delivery dates, warranty periods and so on.

Update your records accordingly after this phase.

CLOSE

Having now negotiated the terms on which you are to do business you now need to ask for the order.

Sales people do actually forget to do this - often to avoid a rejection.

The close situation often happens at a higher management level in the company than where the detailed negotiations have taken place.

Needing a higher authority level to obtain a signature on the contract can be the trigger for the senior management in your organisation to accompany you to help close the sale.

At this critical stage don't hold back, call in any help you feel you need to secure the deal.

ORDER

A salesperson often believes the order is the end of the transaction.

WRONG - it is the beginning!

The follow through to installation, training and support visits should continue to be the responsibility of the salesperson.

This will allow continuity of contact and enable the development of an enduring relationship that will yield future additional business.

REMEMBER the easiest and most profitable business is repeat business.

AND the best new prospects come via the personal referrals of satisfied customers!

Completing your records

The individual prospect records should be updated every time contact is made with your prospect, and each month this information will form the basis of your sales forecasting for the next three months and the foundation for the Company's cash flow forecast.

We have added a simple Sales Prospect Sheet as a paper based example on which you might want to test out your requirements before comparing the electronic programmes on offer and investing in a system.

Your Company	Sales Prospect Sheet	Sales Person:		Page No:
Prospect Name:	Potential Business Products / Services	Value	Forecast Order Date	Probability %
Contact:				
Position:				
Tel No:				
Mobile:				
Email:				
Website:				
Address				

Contact Record	Status of Negotiation	S	P	A	N	C	O	
Date	Record of Contacts	Actions O/S - Completed						Date

There are a myriad of software systems on the market, just run a Google search!

More complex and expensive Customer Relationship Management (CRM) systems are available from giants of the industry such as Salesforce.com and Oracle for managing a company's interactions with customers and sales prospects using database technology to organize, automate, and synchronise the sales process.

In addition these systems have the ability to integrate marketing, customer service and technical support activities.

Successful sales people use such a system *for their own benefit* to instil discipline into their activity and ensure they are well organised to get great results.

How will your Sales Managers view your efforts?

What will they be planning to do?

What action might they take?

Let's get into the Manager's head!

At the month end they will ask the sales team to re-assess their prospects as to their progress through the sales cycle, the probability of achieving the order and to forecast the month of receipt (see Chapter 8: Forecasting).

They will question each salesperson as to the seniority of contact and the level of authority to sign that order.

They will not forget that sales people are notoriously optimistic. Also, the spread of business between the months is very rarely ideal, everything will always be OK in the third or most distant month!

Beware:

They will recognise this as a danger signal that business will slip out further in time and will reduce your revenue forecast in the short term.

They will ensure that each salesperson fills in details of all the most recent activity, especially the contact names, email addresses and telephone numbers.

 If a salesperson then leaves to join a competitor all their SPANCO records are available and either the Sales Manager or the new salesperson can ensure continuity of contact and rapidly carry out a damage limitation exercise.

This data is also useful if a salesperson is ill or on holiday when a potential customer rings up with a query or wants an urgent appointment.

The notes on the record should give a good idea of where the salesperson is in the sales cycle and record any problems that have arisen and are outstanding.

This system, if worked effectively, can be of great assistance in managing a sales oriented business not only for the management but also for the sales force.

Chapter 4: Key Performance Ratios

The next three chapters concentrate on generating leads, qualifying them and building a quality prospect bank for you to work on.

But how many prospects do you need or can effectively handle? This will depend on the type of product or service you are selling and the associated selling cycle timescale.

Key Performance Ratios or Indicators (KPIs)

We are now in the realm of statistics (which vary from person to person and product to product). However, the example below is a good illustration:

> One qualified suspect needs ten phone calls - 1:10
>
> One good prospect comes from five qualified suspects - 1:5
>
> One order comes from three good prospects - 1:3

From these ratios you can see that to gain the three prospects needed to obtain one order you must have 15 qualified suspects and to get that list you would have had to make *150 phone calls*!

These are your Key Performance Ratios.

Every business has these ratios and unless you match or exceed the activity required you will simply NOT hit your targets.

Build up your own set of ratios and compare them with the most successful sales people in the company.

This emphasises the absolute need for disciplined and effective activity if you want to succeed.

Chapter 5: Lead Generation

Every salesperson loves sales leads.

Where do they come from?

The Internet is now almost certainly the greatest source of leads plus a mine of valuable information.

Hopefully your company will have an effective website and you can rely upon a plentiful supply of web enquiries.

It is essential that they also participate fully in the most popular social media scenarios :

Facebook has now exceeded one billion users

Linked In has over 200 million registrations

Twitter has half a billion users

With this degree of participation they cannot be ignored!

It is virtually certain that every one of your prospects will have a website with varying degrees of relevant information but whatever is there - use it.

A great deal can be gleaned from reading the company's Annual Report and from the Chairman's summary you should be able to assess the company's financial health, objectives and future direction.

Having been seen to have done your homework and acquired such knowledge you will rise in your prospects estimation having demonstrated a thorough and professional approach.

Web Enquiries

The advent of email marketing and web enquiries has hastened the contact cycle and the customer often has an instant response expectation.

Given there is so much online competition prompt follow up action is essential.

You may find it useful to have a set of "standard" responses ready for the most frequently received query types.

Always ask the potential customer to call you or let you have their number so you can follow up and qualify the lead. You can then build the relationship on a personal rather than at an electronic level.

Third Party References

These are the best leads of all. A customer who is satisfied with your product or service tells a friend, relative, acquaintance, colleague, someone on the train or their clients about your product or service and refers them to you. You come recommended and there is already an interest.

In such cases there is a tendency to drop everything and rush round.

Instead, telephone the person and qualify them yourself! They are still a suspect, not yet a prospect. Once qualified you are better prepared, set up the appointment and you are off to a great start!

In your conversation there will be plenty of opportunities to refer to such supportive statements (see Chapter 12: Support Statements).

Make sure you use them.

Why not personalise a "Thank You" card or letter and send to the customer who gave you the lead. This is so much more personal than an email. What is more, you could get more leads!

If appropriate take them to lunch - and you may get even more referrals.

In the insurance industry they make a point of actively asking for third party references from their customers.

Why not do the same?

TASK: Design a personally addressed and signed letter or card to existing customers, with incentives for providing third party contacts for new leads.

As with any mailshot, follow it up with a telephone call.

Don't expect others to do your work for you - you have to chase and work at it – that is what selling is all about!

Be disciplined about this activity.

Advertising

It is important that you maintain close links with your marketing department and be aware of any campaigns that your Company is carrying out. Do not let your potential customers be more informed than you.

Also you can feed back the results of their campaigns to them.

Unilever once said that *"50% of our advertising brings results, 50% is useless. The problem is we do not know which is which!"*

Companies spend huge sums on advertising. Work with your advertising department which should mean better quality leads and more of them. If you do not work with your advertising department that means fewer leads and wasted money. This is putting your business at risk.

Log all leads and the results of your telephone calls. This will show:

> If you are getting your fair share of leads.

> The quality of your leads.

> Your ability to turn suspects into prospects (a key performance ratio).

Physical Canvassing

If your territory is in London or a city centre or you have a generalised product then you can canvass on foot. This technique is used less frequently these days as many office receptions are manned by security people for the whole office block but carried out professionally it can still be effective.

Choose a densely populated street or business park. Have your SPANCO system with you and a stock of marketing material. If you have a presentation on your laptop or iPad, take it along.

Walk into the reception, introduce yourself, your name, your Company, your product or service and your reason for calling. Keep it brief!

> Find out the NAME - the person who has:

> the Need for your product or service

> the Authority to sign an order

> the Money (budget) to pay

> the Enthusiasm to sign (once you have met them)

Ask the receptionist to try to get you a few minutes with that person (see Chapter 6: Qualifying Suspects).

The receptionist may also be a rich source of information and even if you do not get put through, the receptionist can be very helpful.

Do not alienate the receptionist. Be polite.

Don't start telling jokes. Most receptionists have heard them all and are busy.

Do not try to sell to the receptionist. They cannot sign.

Always thank the receptionist for any information.

Fill in your SPANCO record with as much data as you can. Pick up leaflets, company reports (ask for one) or newsletters.

You can glean a lot from a company reception.

One important but rarely mentioned factor is the "feel" that you get from physically stepping into the reception.

What is the "energy"' like? Is it old fashioned, dowdy, uncared for, or is it well decorated, cool, expensive? Does it have flowers, bright lights, wall panels, large monitors? Is it busy or dead, welcoming or hostile?

From our research on energy we know that there are three stages of energy which also correspond to the stages of an organisation and their resultant buying habits.

1) **Birth:**   New, vibrant, exciting, starting out, fresh, lots of ideas, creative, open, receptive, looking to the future, going for it.

2) **Sustaining:**   Established, on-going, stable, well organised, lots of rules, protective, conservative, risk averse.

3) **Death:**   Fading, coming towards the final curtain, stuck, blocked, resistant to new ideas, cost cutting, downsizing, mean but not lean, redundancies, tired.

If the company is in Stage 1 you may have struck lucky. If the company is in Stage 2 they have probably already heard of you and may already be supplied by one of your competitors.

If the company is in Stage 3 then unless you can offer them huge savings or you are a Company Receiver, your chances of an order are minimal.

However from death comes rebirth so you may strike lucky if they have just appointed a new CEO, with the power to save the company, and you manage to get an appointment.

If you get past reception it may be to see the NAME or to do some fact finding with someone lower down but who can give you valuable information. They may have a few minutes to spare.

If you don't ask you don't get!

If you don't get past reception, leave a brochure, your card and perhaps an invitation to an exhibition or a demonstration.

Ask the receptionist to give these to the NAME and to say that you will be phoning in a few days time.

Make a point of this and be pleasant and polite to the receptionist.

Diary a few days ahead and telephone for an appointment, hopefully the receptionist will remember you.

Advantage of a visit:	You get a feel for the company
Disadvantage:	You can waste a lot of time

Telephone Canvassing

Again, you are looking for information. Type of business. The NAME.
Is the business buoyant or depressed?   Potential need for your product?

To canvass by phone, use the most appropriate source of contacts for your type of business:

Websites

Social media - Linked In, Twitter, Facebook

Yellow pages, online, local editions

Trade journals

Local newspapers

Voicemail - the curse of the telephone canvasser!

Be prepared to go through to voicemail, have your succinct message ready, who you are, who you represent, why you are calling, your telephone number and, if convenient when you will call again.

If you believe they are a good prospect, keep trying.

Mailshots

In addition to emailing why not compose a letter* with the advantages and benefits of your product or service and send it to suspects unearthed above.

Emails are now so often caught up in spam or anti-virus systems the old fashioned letter is making a comeback!

Try inserting a reply paid card and either:

1) Sit back and wait for the cards to roll in. The normal return is 1% or 2% so don't hold your breath!

or

2) Telephone and qualify

No good? Then say goodbye. Do not waste time trying to sell to someone who has no Need, Authority, Money, or Enthusiasm.

Possible Prospect? Get an appointment.

Dependant on the nature of your business and your key ratios, the number of emails, mailshots and telephone calls required can vary significantly.

 If you have a large key ratio i.e. 20 calls to get one appointment you may consider:

a) Telephone techniques training

b) Getting a telephone salesperson to do the qualifying for you and to get appointments. This frees you to carry out the important face to face appointments with qualified prospects.

 Telephone sales people are usually paid at a cheaper rate than a top salesperson (which you are!).

Exhibitions

These are expensive to attend, to run and are very time consuming but if well organised can give you valuable face to face time with prospects and the ability to demonstrate your products and services.

Try to arrange an appointment there and then.

Prompt follow up is essential as those same prospects will have also visited your competitor's stands!

It is not within our remit to discuss how to organise exhibitions, however in the Appendix section we have listed a whole list of useful tips should you find yourself working on the company stand.

Make it enjoyable – remember the infectious nature of enthusiasm!

Chapter 6: Qualifying Suspects

You now have a long list of people who you suspect may need you product or service. To convert them into prospects you need to qualify them.

How do you do this?

As referred to in the last chapter, you are looking for the N A M E - the person who has:

1.   **N** - The Need for your product

2.   **A** - The Authority to sign an order

3.   **M** - The Money to pay

4.   **E** - The Enthusiasm to buy

All these criteria may not exist in one person, for example if you are selling a sales training course:-

1.   The need will be in the sales force.

2.   The authority may be with the Sales Manager or Sales Director.

3.   The money may come out of the sales budget controlled by the Sales Director or the training budget controlled by the Personnel Director or even a separate fund controlled by the Finance Director.

4.   The enthusiasm may be present in some but not all.

Finding the first three requires detective work.

Generating the fourth requires sales ability.

Needs

In Chapter 2 we dealt with Features Advantages and Benefits. Your product knowledge will tell you the features of your product.

You have listed the features, asked the question "so what?" for each feature and listed the corresponding advantage - so far so good.

Now you must determine the needs of your customer.

This can only be done by probing. By asking questions you get to understand the needs of your customer.

Chapter 13: Asking Questions deals with this subject in more detail.

Needs are often associated with problems. Needs are a lack of a solution, your product or service may provide the answer.

Example: I have a headache. I cannot get rid of it. I have a problem.

You may sell me an aspirin or a shiatsu massage. Both will satisfy my needs of getting rid of a headache but in different ways.

The same need can be satisfied by different solutions.

Another example :

My need to get from home to work can be satisfied by walking, cycling, taxi, bus, train, car or plane.

Needs and Wants

Advertising can be a sophisticated method of creating needs, some of which are "false needs". A false need is a "want".

I may want a Ferrari but I do not need one. A smaller, less glamorous car will get me from A to B for less outlay but it will not satisfy my ego.

Fish and chips will assuage my hunger. Cordon Bleu however may not, but such fine cuisine may fulfil my need and want for other things like presentation, taste and style.

Because many wants are related to self-actualisation in a world where other needs are fulfilled, they become very strong. Some people are trendy, fashion slaves and will spend more on clothes and jewellery than on food.

This is because they have **disposable income**.

 This is money you earn that is above the amount required to satisfy the basics of life i.e. food, water, shelter and warmth.

It is important, in retail selling especially, to determine if your product is bought with basic or disposable income, for it will be marketed and sold in different ways.

Latent Needs

The good salesperson can sell when the customer does not initially see the need for your product or service.

 If selling was purely the satisfaction of obvious needs there would be no sales activity required because customers would be very clear what they want and ask for it. As a salesperson you would be out of a job!

However if your product or service is innovative -such as facility management or a category of outsourcing - then your sales presentation will point out the deficiencies with the current system and the advantages and benefits of using your solution.

You have thus created a need, where one did not previously exist, in the consciousness of your customer.

Authority

The critical person you are looking for is the one who has the authority and the power to sign an order. They are usually in charge of a budget.

In large organisations budgets may be administered centrally but in smaller companies there is usually less rigour in applying rules and budget responsibilities may be hazy and not clearly laid out.

In partnerships all parties are jointly and severally liable so one partner can sign on behalf of others. This is worth remembering if, when you come to get your order signed, the partner you are dealing with has gone on a month's leave – get hold of another partner – they can sign!

Some people may sign an order but not have the authority. That is your customer's problem not yours. However in the interest of a long term relationship you may need to take this into consideration should you get into this situation.

In all cases you need to ask questions to determine the approval process.

Money

Who has the budget? Is there a budget? Can we create one? Is it controlled by an individual or a committee?

How far up the hierarchical tree do you need to go? If the need is strong enough will money be found? When does the financial year start?

Is there a contingency fund that the Financial Director may have tucked away for emergencies or for 'must have' products like the one that you are selling?

 All you have to do now is to persuade your customer how important your product or service is, and that they cannot afford to do business without it!

These are the sort of questions that many sales people often do not ask.

However all your sales efforts and presentations may be in vain if the customer cannot pay for your offerings. Therefore these questions should be asked early on in the sale or you may end up wasting your time.

 In many companies if the need plus the benefits are great enough the money will be found. If that is so, concentrate on creating the need before asking for the money; always establish the need first.

Remember that you may also be competing with other needs for a slice of the same budget so make your case a strong one.

Discounts

This can be dealt with in the negotiating phase but if early on in the sale you see problems on budget then start thinking how you can tackle them. Be prepared. Learn how to sell without discounts, use only as a final close if needed!

Be creative if you have to discount. Link them to further orders or give them retrospective monthly discounts if they sign today for an annual contract.

This ensures a mutually beneficial, long term business partnership that keeps out your competitors.

Delayed payments

Can you bridge payments over two tax or financial years?

This is a creative way of compromising in March / April or for December / January orders.

Enthusiasm

This is what it is all about!

If you are not enthusiastic about your product then how can you expect the prospect to be?

Enthusiasm is infectious.

Ensure that you know your product thoroughly, learn how to sell it, work hard and your enthusiasm will do the rest.

Remember - when all else is equal the enthusiastic salesperson will get the order!

Chapter 7: The Prospect Bank

Once you have qualified your prospects you need to collect them all together.

This is your prospect bank.

The number of prospects in your bank depends on the length of your sales cycle (see Chapter 4: Key Performance Ratios).

If your sales cycle is short you should have a larger bank because turnover will be rapid.

If the sales cycle is long, prospects will remain in your bank for some time AND there will be a limit to the number you can effectively manage at any one time.

In these cases you may wish to monitor any company changes and web updates for interesting new content relating to your prospect - news stories, company announcements, launches, exhibitions and blogs.

Google Alerts are one of the systems available where emails are sent to you when Google finds new content that matches your search input.

This can also be an excellent way of keeping an eye on competitors and for developments occurring in your particular business sector.

Definition of a prospect

A prospect is a suspect that you have qualified as a potential customer with a defined need and that you expect to successfully close within your average sales cycle. For example if your average sales cycle is three months then any potential customer that you expect to close within three months goes into your prospect bank.

Hot Prospects

These would be prospects that you expect to close within the next month of a three monthly cycle.

Why have a prospect bank?

As you close orders so you have to replace the prospects or you will run out and in three months time you will "dry up".

In Chapter 4 on Key Performance Ratios, you will have looked at the relationship between the number of leads that you need to generate in order to keep your prospect bank "topped up".

This is crucial or your income and the revenue of your company will be erratic. This gives you a problem in paying your mortgage and could give your company a cash flow problem!

Reviewing your Prospect Bank

Another use of the prospect bank is to expose "old chestnuts". These are companies that appear for long periods in your prospect bank and do not shift. They need weeding out or the subject of drastic action.

It may be comforting for the future to have a large prospect bank but if you are not going to convert them into orders you are just kidding yourself!

If a prospect falls into the "old chestnut" category you may need to re-appraise them as a prospect and take them off your list or take someone else in, say a manager or director in an attempt to "up the stakes" or get a second opinion.

You may use this as an opportunity to go higher up the hierarchy than your present contact who may be blocking you.

You should thoroughly review your prospect bank regularly. Be honest and ruthless with your pruning, do not let an unconvinced customer waste your valuable time.

Classifying prospects

You need to classify each prospect according to the percentage chance of closing that particular order (see table in Chapter 8: Forecasting).

Multiply the value of the order by the percentage chance and enter that in the Forecast column. Be realistic. Consult your SPANCO records to see where you are in the sale process and how much more work you have left to do.

Target high potential outstanding appointments, if you have identified a need, do not delay and allow a competitor an opening!

Like you, they are always looking for new opportunities, and if they get there before you, they could close the order before you have even made an appointment.

Chapter 8: Forecasting

Let's start off with an explanation and a definition.

Forecasting is an attempt to predict the future. It could be a weather forecast, a business forecast or a forecast on a horse race or football match.

Risk and uncertainty are central to forecasting and prediction.

Definition: *Forecasting is the process of making statements about events whose actual outcomes have not yet been observed.*

It is considered good practice to indicate the degree of uncertainty attached to a forecast. In all cases, the input data must be accurate and as up to date as possible; otherwise your forecast will have no value.

GIGO: We have all heard of GIGO. It stands for **Garbage In, Garbage Out**. In other words, and especially on a computer, the value and accuracy of a forecast is directly related to the value and accuracy of the data that we put into the computer. If we put in unreliable, out of date, inaccurate information, then the computer will spew out rubbish.

IOIO: Hopefully, your forecasts will be IOIO ones. This stands for**: Information In, Information Out**. This means that you enter up to date, unbiased, accurate facts, and as a result your forecast is up to date, unbiased, and accurate. This enables people to **TRUST YOU**.

In Sales, trust is highly important. If your customer trusts you and your manager trusts you, then you are almost home and dry. Whatever happens, do not lie, or falsify your forecast. It may be tempting, but you will always be found out!   *Trust is hard to build and so easy to lose*.

All companies selling products or services require a monthly forecast from each salesperson and YOU need to create it for your own purposes, with particular reference to YOUR commission and cash flow!

In large organisations the National Sales Manager will amalgamate regional and area forecasts to produce a National Sales Forecast. These figures will be sent to the Finance department, manufacturing division, the importers and the distribution channels. This enables all of them to plan their future operations.

You can now see the importance of your forecast and the need for realism.

Sales people are notoriously optimistic, so using a percentage probability is a useful tool. It bridges the gap between perception and reality!

See the example below for a Monthly prospect list. We have only put in five prospects in this simple example with one order already confirmed.

Hopefully you have many more! If not, get on the phone and get some appointments!

Prospect List		Month	
Name	Order Value	% Chance	Forecast
Acme Holdings	7,500	90	6,750
A Prospect Ltd	6,000	60	3,600
Green Bank	6,750	80	5,400
Rich Oil Co	8,000	30	2,400
A Farmer	5,950	100	5,950
TOTAL	34,200		24,100
		AVERAGE ORDER VALUE	4,820

In the example above, you will see that, according to you, there is a 90% chance of getting the Acme Holdings order by the end of the month. So, instead of handing in a forecast of 7,500, you downsize Acme to 6,750. These are not true figures. They are relative figures.

You also reckon that you may have to work harder on A Prospect Ltd and so you downgrade the expected order to 60% chance from 6,000 to 3,600.

Work your way through the table using this process.

By adding all the values of the percentage orders forecast at the beginning of the month you can calculate the expected order value for the end of the month. If you divide this total by the number of orders taken, this will give you an **average order value**. This is a useful tool for forecasting.

A Forecast is a snapshot in time. It is continually changing due to the activity that takes place during the month. If you do nothing, your prospect may go off the boil and you will not get the order.

However if you pester your prospect they may get irritated and go elsewhere, as they dislike pressure selling. You need to know the likes and dislikes of your prospect. The more understanding you have of your prospects, the more appropriately your treatment of them and the more accurate your forecast.

Sales managers usually hold weekly meetings to review each salesperson's activity, and then upgrade or downgrade their forecast as the month progresses. Hopefully the ups and downs will cancel each other out.

Often, the more prospects that you have in your Prospect Bank, the more accurate your forecast will be, as statistically you have more options to juggle!

Sales people who are on the ball quickly replace their cancellations with new prospects. By the end of the month, if you have done your job properly, the figures will have balanced out to achieve the result in your original forecast.

If you have your own business and Banks or Investors have lent money to you then your ability to forecast accurately will enhance your credibility significantly.

Nobody likes unpleasant surprises!

This process is very simplistic and may well need significant refining dependent upon the type of business, value, and volume of orders.

However, do check how accurate you are over the next few months and adjust your percentage up or down accordingly. BEWARE of over optimism.

With practice your forecasting accuracy will improve and experience gained will enable you to focus on what is important and what is not.

Sales people who forecast reliably and accurately
are highly valued.

Chapter 9: Telephoning for Appointments

There are two situations where telephoning for appointments makes sense.

1.   Your product or service is specialised, perhaps in a niche market.

Few people have need of it. In which case you use the telephone to search out and qualify your suspects.

You do not necessarily have to speak to the NAME to do this.

Many people in the organisation can give you the information on needs, processes and budget allocation. If the suspect passes these first "tests" and "qualifies" to go on your prospect list, you THEN need to get an appointment with the NAME.

2.   Your product or service is needed by everybody.

Here, little qualification is required and the sale hinges on you getting an appointment with the NAME. You may well have several competitors, as the market is huge, so the better you are on the telephone the more chance you have of getting an appointment and a sale.

Prior to phoning for an appointment find out as much as you can about your customer.

This may be their buying habits, budgets, who buys what. Who is their existing supplier? Have they ever used your product or service before?

Have all this information on your SPANCO system and have a copy of the brochure or mailshot that you previously sent out, in front of you.

Preparation is 90% of the process here.

Telephoning

Please refer to the Telephone Selling Skills graphics outlined in the Appendices, or visit our website. Use this guide to make up your own telephone script and use it regularly.

This is how it works:

1.   Greeting and identification.

"Hello, my name is …………from …………… (name your Company)

We are ……………(state what your company is known as e.g. management consultants, shipbuilders, specialist engineers, an advertising agency)

We specialise in …………….(state what your company does or makes e.g. leadership training, building luxury yachts to order, engineering solutions, producing eye catching websites)"

2.   State the purpose of your call.

"May I speak to NAME (the person that you need to make an appointment with)?"

3. Take the initiative.

"Are they in?"

a) If the answer is *"Yes"* say *"Would you put me through please?"*

If you are put through, repeat the greeting and identification to the NAME and start selling!

b) If the answer is *"No, the NAME is not in his/her office"* say *"Are they in the building?"*

If the answer is *"Yes"* say *"What extension are they on? Would you put me through please?"*

If the answer is "*Yes; I'll put you through*." and the NAME answers the phone go back to **1. Greeting and Identification**, and start selling!

If the answer is "*No, they are not in the building*." Or "*No, I cannot put you through, they are in a meeting*." say "*When will they be available, please?*"

At this point you may be put through to the NAME's secretary or PA. If so go back to **1. Greeting and Identification**, say that you are following up an e-mail, or letter and that you wish to make an appointment to discuss the matter further.

Ask when the NAME is next available (Assumptive Close) and say "*Would next Wednesday or Thursday be convenient?*" (Alternative Close). See a number of different closing techniques in Chapter 16: Closing the Sale.

Say "*I will require about 30 minutes, but this may extend to 45 minutes if a discussion ensues, or there are any questions*."

If the secretary refuses or procrastinates or is uncertain say "*This is an important meeting, may I suggest that we make a provisional appointment for Wednesday at 10am and if that is not convenient you may phone me back with an alternative?*"

If the answer is "*No*" then you say - "*May I leave a message for NAME to say that I have called and to phone me back next week with a convenient time to meet? I'll give you my details again: My phone number is xxxxxxxx*" (Assumptive Close).

Thank the secretary/PA and hang up.

If the secretary/PA accepts your previous suggestion for an appointment say "*Thank You, just to confirm, the appointment is Wednesday at 10 am for 45 minutes*"

Thank the secretary/PA again and hang up.

It is **crucial** that you follow now this up with a confirmation letter or e-mail.

As you can see, you remain polite at all times, you do not make inappropriate jokes, you doggedly pursue the appointment and you thank the receptionist, secretary or PA for helping you.

If they try to block you then use the techniques for handling objections in Chapter 15.

The appendix has a diagram of this conversation that you can refer to and personalise. The diagram is also on our website. The purpose is to show how at each stage you could easily be put off by a junior member of staff in your customer's organisation and easily lose out on a valuable order!

Your NAME could also lose out. They may need your product and never know!

Bear in mind that your PROSPECT may have a *latent need* i.e. they are unaware that they have a need for your product or service. Until they have found out about what you are offering they remain ignorant and will not reap the benefits.

Once you have established that they have a latent need and that your product or service fulfils it, then the rest is easy.

The biggest struggle may be getting the appointment with the NAME so it is worth spending time working on ways to penetrate their defences.

If you don't, your competitor will!

Also the NAME will know more about their organisation's problems and needs than people lower down the hierarchy being accountable for solving them.

Without seeing you, they will never realise the cost savings, time savings, better quality and other benefits that your product or service can offer them.

Therefore it is imperative that you get that appointment!

Chapter 10: Face to Face

Your telephone techniques have worked. You have your first appointment, well done.

What should you do next?

Go searching

Now you have the names of your attendees find out as much as possible - look them up on Facebook, Linked In - and search other social networks. They may have hobbies or a sporting affiliation matching that of your own that will build rapport.

What are the company's latest Tweets?

Check their website for news items and, where available, read the company's Annual Report and the Chairman's statement

Do your homework it will pay dividends!

Now set your Objectives

What do you want to get out of this meeting?

Put together your hierarchy of objectives.

 A signed order for mega bucks

 A small but modest toe in the door pilot scheme order

 Permission for you to carry out a survey

 Introductions to key people

 A date in the future for you to present your proposal

Arousal of interest - will talk to others on your behalf

Will put you on list of preferred or approved suppliers

Will put you on file for future reference

Wants to be kept in touch with new developments

Prepare a Checklist

How will you present your information?

On an iPad, laptop, large monitor, projector.

Internet Link / Wi-Fi

Flip chart

Video

Match your visual aids to the size of the audience.

How many people in this meeting?

Remember to phone beforehand and ask about the size of room and how much time you have been allotted?

Is your presentation a specially organised meeting, or is it part of a board meeting where other business will be discussed?

If this is the case you need *to be on time and not run over* your allotted schedule.

Be prepared to be cut short, so make your presentation brief and ensure you get across the key points. You can always expand during the questions that follow.

What equipment will you need?

What equipment will your prospect provide? Many companies have their own visual aid systems so all you have to do is plug into their system. Remember to have the right connector and format e.g. USB flash drive and DVD with you.

Where ever possible do a trial run through to avoid embarrassing glitches on the day.

Do not over present. Using a sledgehammer to crack a nut can be embarrassing for all concerned. Equally do not under present. Don't come out thinking "If only I had …. this with me, done X or Y"

Know how much time do you have been allocated and appreciate these are busy people, so **NEVER** run over - leave time for questions - yours as well as theirs.

Highlight the main messages you need to get over within that time and align these to the meeting objectives you have set yourself.

Look smart and professional

Your prospect will be watching you closely so:

> Brush up your presentation skills

> Establish rapport

> Establish empathy

> Be genuine

REMEMBER

You never get a second chance to make a first impression

In our next book "**Successful Selling: Advanced Techniques**", currently in preparation, we discuss the use of neuro-linguistic programming (NLP) in sales situations.

People learn NLP because it gives them the tools and the insights to become much improved and influential communicators. It allows them to feel more in charge of themselves and enhancing their effectiveness in their business environment.

We will be covering the following NLP topics in detail:

Rapport - enabling you to appreciate the other person's map of the world.

Matching, pacing and leading.

Behaviours that convey respect, empathy and genuineness.

When it is appropriate to show your feelings.

REMEMBER

People cannot read our minds, only our behaviour.

Chapter 11: Opening the Sale

Greetings and Identification

When you first make contact with a prospect you greet them, tell them your name, the company you work for, the position you hold in that company and the reason why you have contacted them.

It is amazing how many sales people forget to do this and jump straight into the sales presentation.

An example of greeting and identification is:

"Good morning Mr Smith, My name is .... I am the Account Executive for XYZ Engineering Limited. I would like to introduce you to our services. "

Scope for improvement? . . .

Initial Advantage Statement

An Initial Advantage Statement should give the top level advantage enjoyed by your services that relate specifically to this customer.

Just saying *"I would like to introduce you to our services"* is a touch weak.

Think of the ways that you can open the sales conversation.

Example:

"Many companies are looking to increase the return on their existing assets. At XYZ Engineering we have produced a support package that will enable you to maximise your production by significantly reducing machine downtime."

Note that in the example above the top level advantage of *"increasing the return on your assets"* is linked to a specific benefit *"maximising your production by significantly reducing machine downtime"*.

TASK: Write down three Initial Advantage Statements relevant to you. Try them out, always work to improve them.

Read them out to your colleagues.

Discuss other possible Initial Advantage Statements. By doing this you are sharing ideas and improving your own skills and those of your sales team.

Everybody wins!

Chapter 12: Support Statements

Support statements occur when you hear a customer make a favourable comment about your product.

The formula is:

1. Agree with the customer

2. Bring in or expand on the benefit the customer has enjoyed

For example:

Customer: *"(your Company) has a good name in this market"*.

Salesperson: *"I agree. We are the market leader. This is because we are the most experienced company and can offer you the best service"*.

Sales people who use support statements get more orders than those who don't. Support statements build rapport with the customer.

Using the example in the previous Chapter, the salesperson gave the advantage that their service was capable of "*significantly reducing machine downtime.*" Let us suppose that the prospect thought that this was a good thing and said "*Hmm, that would be good!*"

At this point you could probe for more information by asking questions such as "*It seems that you have a problem regarding downtime. Can you tell me more?*" This is a directive probe (see Chapter 13: Asking Questions) .

 The reason you would probe now is to get more information to expose a customer need so that you can bring in the appropriate benefits of your service. This is great but you have missed an opportunity to give a support statement.

You therefore need to

1.   give a support statement

2.   let it sink in

3.   and then use a probe.

REMEMBER: Every time that you support and agree with the prospect you build more rapport and make them feel good.

Here is an example support statement that you could use:

"Yes, you are right. Imagine that by using our system you could drastically reduce the machine downtime and radically improve the production figures. That would really be maximising your assets!"

Then you can choose to probe more such as:

"Tell me more about the causes of your downtime and I will produce a proposal as to how we can best help you."

But hang on; have you built sufficient rapport yet? If not, make a note "reduce machine downtime"' in your benefit bank to come back to later in the discussion. A hard sell now may make the customer resistant.

So what next ?

Try a non-directive probe such as *"What other problems do you have with your production schedules?"* This is an open question and invites the prospect to talk about what they want to talk about rather than what you want to talk about.

By doing this they think that they are retaining power and therefore can afford to relax their guard and talk more freely. They feel in control.

Chapter 13: Asking Questions

A lot of selling consists of asking questions. **Selling** is not **telling**.

You need to find out what the customer's response is to your initial advantage statement and also to ascertain the customer's needs.

Whenever you make an initial advantage statement or a claim for your product the customer will react in one of three different ways:

Positive: accepts what you say and is interested

Negative: rejects what you say and is not interested

Indifferent: does not care either way

If the prospect is positive you need to support him (see Chapter 12: Support Statements).

If they are negative or indifferent you need to find out why.

You also need to find out as much relevant information as possible about the prospect so that you can work out his/her needs and match them with the features and advantages of your product or service.

To do this it is necessary to ask questions. There are two types of questions:

1. Directive (closed) Questions:

This is where you direct the customer into an area that you, the salesperson, wants to talk about.

 An example of a directive question is: *"Are you interested in x?"* The only answers to a directive question are *"Yes"* or *"No"*.

This is why they are also referred to as closed questions as you have closed down the response to *"Yes"* or *"No"*.

2. Indirect (open) Questions:

Indirect questions allow the customer to talk about what they want to talk about rather than what you want to talk about. From such a conversation the salesperson may indirectly ascertain the customer's needs.

 To help you remember examples of indirect questions use the rhyme:

I have six good friends both rare and true, they are

> 1. *'What?'*
>
> 2. *'Where?'*
>
> 3. *'How?'*
>
> 4. *'When?'*
>
> 5. *'Why?'*
>
> 6. *'Who?'*

If you use too many direct questions in succession it will seem like a "third degree" and you may not get anywhere.

 If you feel this is what is happening, switch to indirect or open questions in order to release the deadlock.

In the previous Chapter we gave examples of direct or closed questions:

"Can I produce a proposal as to how best we can help you?"

Here the customer can either answer *"Yes, that would be a good idea"* or *"No thank you, not at this stage."*

To prevent this and a possible deadlock, we suggested the use of an indirect or open question:

"What other problems do you have with your production schedules?"

Here the customer feels less threatened and is free to talk about his/her problems thus providing you with useful information for your proposal.

In this case there is genuine dialogue rather than the customer having to face a barrage of directive questions.

Letting the customer talk is why you have two ears and only one mouth.

In selling you need to listen twice as much as you talk.

If the customer asks you a question, that is a different matter.

However keep your answer brief and to the point.

Do not go off on a tangent or you will confuse the customer and the sale will lose focus.

Chapter 14: Proof Statements

Proof statements occur when a customer does not believe what you have said or questions the validity of your claim.

The customer does not think that the product or service can achieve what you say it can.

In such cases you:

1. Rephrase the customer's doubts and

2. Offer proof in the form of a demonstration or third party references.

Here is an example taken from the previous chapter:

Customer: *"Well, I don't believe that by introducing your systems you can reduce downtime on our machines!"*

Salesperson: *"Hmm, I can understand your doubts. However we have many satisfied customers on our books who originally thought the same. Now they are enjoying all the benefits of reduced downtime and increased production.*

Take ABC Engineering for example. Here are their before and after figures. You can see the incredible improvement. Also take this list of satisfied customers. You are very welcome to phone them and discuss how we helped each one of them.

 With our systems in place you could be reaping similar rewards for your own company."

As you can see, establishing a selection of quality third party references will add value within your selling process.

Alternatively:

Salesperson: *"Yes I can see why you have doubts, but we can prove it right here. Let us carry out an initial survey on Section 1 and we will reduce your machine downtime by a minimum of 15%. That will validate our claims and prove that our systems really work.*

We can then work with you to install our systems across your whole manufacturing unit with similar results. You cannot lose. But you can make some huge gains!"

Proof statements are an important part of the Sales Process in boosting customer confidence in your ability to perform and to keep your promises.

Chapter 15: Handling Objections

Many sales people fear objections. However, remember this. Every time you overcome an objection you are one step closer to the sale!

The more objections that you can overcome the more likely the customer will buy. There are bound to be objections that a customer will find in every product or service so do NOT try to avoid them or they will come back later and could sabotage the sale.

In fact the most successful sales people already know what the objections are likely to be and PRE - HANDLE them.

There are two types of objections, easy and difficult.

1. Easy objections: This is when you have the answer to the objection.

For example: the customer wants to buy a red car and you have demonstrated a green one. The customer objects to the colour.

This is an easy objection to overcome as you have a red car out the back. You could say: *"Oh that's no problem. We have a red car in stock. Come and have a look."*

You could however, use a Sharp Angle Close at this point (see Chapter 16: Closing the Sale).

"If I can locate one for you will you go ahead and place an order?"

2. Hard objections: This is when you have no solution to the customer's objection.

For example your price is too high and you cannot discount any further. Or you haven't got a red car to sell. What you do now is:

1. Refine the objection

2. List all the benefits of your product

3. Try closing for the order

Refine: "Obviously a bright colour is an important feature in your choice of car, and we have some new and extremely attractive colours in this model that has the full specification that you have requested."

List: "This one, for example does 0-60 in six seconds. It also has traction control making it fast round corners as well as on the straight, which was something that you were particularly interested in. It also has all the following features that you stated were important in making the right decision. Let's run through the list: ......"

Close for the Order: "As you can see these two models are perfect for your needs. Do you want to take the British Racing Green or the Liquid Yellow?" (see the next Chapter for the many different types of closes).

Try this: Learning how to refine objections is one of the most important parts in handling objections.

 List the most common objections that you get and refine them. The more the better!

 Share them with your colleagues and you will be better prepared, your skills will improve and you will get more orders.

Chapter 16: Closing the Sale

Many sales people shy away from actually closing the sale in case the customer says "No!"

Understandably they fear rejection.

BUT, in fact, the more times you close, the more likely you are to succeed.

Every time you close and the customer says "No!" it is usually because they have an objection. As we found out earlier, the more objections you can resolve the closer you get to the order.

Failed closes are terrific - yes really!

They unearth previously unexpressed objections. You can now deal with the objection and get on with the job of closing the sale!

Closing a sale has three distinct stages:

1. Assume the sale has been made.

2. List the benefits.

3. Ask for the order

There are many different types of closes. Here are some to add to your repertoire together with examples:

1. The Assumptive Close

All good closes assume that you have got the order, the appointment, or whatever you are trying to achieve.

By assuming, rather than asking, you put the prospect in the potentially awkward situation that they have to disagree with your assumption, or go against you.

Most people prefer to avoid conflict. BUT beware, there are some people who thrive on conflict!

Do not "railroad" the customer or you will cause resentment. Always let the customer 'buy' rather than force a sale. When a customer buys from you they feel in control, which they will like. They feel that is they who are making the decisions, not you.

This is very important and takes great skill on your part. You can only achieve this if you have previously established empathy and rapport earlier in the sale. The close can only take place when you have reached this stage.

Remember it is very difficult to try and pick an unripe apple from a tree. Timing is all important!

Example: *"When you install this machine you will increase productivity and decrease downtime drastically."* Here you are assuming they will install the machine. You then go on to list the benefits, as required in stage 2 of the close.

Ensure that the benefits you list are ones that you have previously agreed with your customer, and have been entered in their "Benefit Bank."

IMPORTANT:

Do not, at this stage, talk about any other benefits or introduce any new ones that you have not previously discussed. That will only confuse the customer and may bring up objections that otherwise would not have arisen. You will then lose the "flow" and, possibly, the order.

Having listed the appropriate benefits you then go on to ask for the order.

2. The Alternative Close

This is where you give the prospect the possibility of choosing between two alternatives.

In fact, both these alternatives are beneficial to you and to your prospect, because the product is beneficial to them, otherwise you would not be selling it!

Example: *"I would like to come and see you to discuss the service in more detail. Which would you prefer, next Wednesday afternoon or Thursday morning?"*

 Note that you have assumed that you will be given the appointment; all the customer needs to do is to decide between the two alternatives.

Here are two more examples:

a)   *"Would you prefer the red car or the green one?"*

This assumes that your customer will buy the car; all they have to do is choose the colour! They are making the decision!

b)   *"I require your signature here. Would you prefer to use your pen or mine?"*

Here, the prospect is cheekily being asked to make a small decision (which pen they use to sign the order).

The big decision i.e. will they actually sign the order? has already been assumed.

3. The Sharp Angle Close

Here, as the salesperson, you are asked if you can supply a specific product, feature or benefit.

Instead of saying *"Yes"* which is rather tame, or saying *"I'll find out"* which betrays a lack of product knowledge, you ask the $64,000 question: *"If I can supply it, will you buy it?"* Obviously not always quite as blatant as that! Although sometimes that approach actually works.

Example: *"Do you have this model in red?"* Instead of saying *"Yes"* or *"I'll go and have a look"* the salesperson replies: *"If I can locate one for you, will you go ahead?"*

It is quite difficult for the customer to say *"No"*, as they have just expressed a need and basically you, as the salesperson, are saying *"If I can fulfil your previously stated need, does that mean you will buy my product?"*

4. Balance Sheet Close

Sometimes a prospect finds it difficult to make a decision. In order to help them, you construct a "Winston Churchill Balance Sheet".

Using Winston Churchill as the example, the salesperson says:

"During the Second World War Winston Churchill had to make some tough decisions. In order to get to the right decision he used to list all the points for, and all the points against, a particular course of action.

He listed them in two columns: FOR and AGAINST. Once he had written them down he added up the total for each and the column with the biggest total was the course of action that he chose. We can do this now".

If you have an indecisive customer, you can list all the benefits from your Benefit Bank in an impressively long "FOR" column. You then list all the objections, which you have previously handled, in the "AGAINST" column. Keeping this short so that when you come to add them up, the "FORS" will be greater than the "AGAINSTS".

Also all the "AGAINSTS" have been nullified in your sales presentation. Faced with this list the customer quickly perceives that the decision is a "no brainer".

5. Puppy Dog Close

A pet shop owner in New York used to sell a record number of puppies. When asked how he did it, he replied:

"When the family are in the shop and they cannot make a decision, I ask them if they would like to take the puppy home and try it out for a week? They usually jump at the chance.

Then a week later, I knock at their door and say 'I am here to take the puppy away. The kids start crying and plead with their parents to keep the puppy. Even Mum and Dad cannot bear to part with it. They look into the puppy's soulful eyes and reach for their purse or their wallet!
I sell loads of puppies that way!"

It was not long before sales people caught on. At Xerox we would install a photocopier on a seven day trial. Within that week it had become indispensable! There was no way they would let us take it away. The copier was sold and so was the customer.

Which of your product or services are you selling using the puppy dog close? What others could be packaged and sold in this way? Why not suggest ways to your marketing department?

Bose, who make high quality, beautiful but expensive stereos, originally made the majority of their sales using this technique and still do.

They did not sell from shops. They used the puppy dog technique in adverts placed in quality newspapers and magazines. Once people had experienced the quality of sound they were reluctant to give it up. The pill was sweetened by breaking the price into four affordable monthly payments.

 By direct marketing in this way they saved many overheads and established a credible market presence.

6. The Benefit Close

During your conversation with the prospective customer you will have been using probing techniques in order to identify your customer's needs. The objective was to match the features of your product or service with the corresponding advantages and to see if these advantages were of any benefit to the customer. If they were, you added them to the benefit bank.

You are now going to close the order.

Pick the three benefits in your benefit bank that will have the strongest impact.

 If you use more, you risk overplaying your hand and the customer may get distracted from the main thrust, which is to get the order signed.

 All closes should include the benefits to the customer of purchasing and owning your product or purchasing and using your service.

Here goes:

"We agreed that when you use our service it will bring you many benefits. It will drastically reduce the time taken to manufacture your product (Benefit 1).

This will provide you with corresponding cost savings of £x000 (Benefit 2) and the ease of use will increase productivity, boost operator confidence and increase morale (Benefit 3).

All you need to do now is to sign the order and we will arrange for the installation. Because we have our own dedicated team, we can do this within three weeks, in line with your requirements.

As you can see from the figures, you have made a good decision as it provide you with an immediate return on investment."

The above close uses three classic benefits:

    1. Speed

    2. Cost savings

    3. Ease of use

The close is also an assumptive close; it includes the phrase "when you use our service" assuming they will.

It also includes two support statements:

1. *"Because we have our own dedicated team, we can do this within three weeks, in line with your requirements."*

2. *"As you can see from the figures, you have made a good decision, as it provides you with an immediate return on investment."*

IMPORTANT: As the salesperson you are more customer facing than your marketing department. You are the eyes and ears of your company.

You are the front-line, the customer interface, so you have important information to impart.

The most successful companies are those where the marketing and sales departments work closely together!

Genuine feedback is a precious commodity, a gift; hopefully the more enlightened marketing departments will say a big Thank You!

There are many other types of close, many of which are specific to your product or service. Talk to your colleagues regarding their favourite closes.

Make sure that they fit comfortably with your ethics, and try them out.

This book is about selling so you will expect us to be selling to you. Let us not disappoint!

In fact when you book one of our sales training courses you will:

be introduced to many new closing techniques

have the opportunity to try them out in structured role plays

learn how to quickly establish rapport and empathy with your customers

be able to classify objections and handle them with ease

know when to support customers to make the right decision (to buy from you)

understand how to open the sale

know the difference between an advantage and a benefit

know when to use proof statements and how to offer third party references

create a compelling sales presentation

learn how to write powerful proposals that maximise sales

organise your diary and prospecting to maximum advantage

learn how to measure and improve your KPIs (Key Performance Indicators)

and much more!

Did we hear you *say:*

"Can I increase my earnings through additional sales, greater commission, and bigger bonuses? Can I win competitions and get promotion?"

Our answer would be:

"If we show you how to, will you visit our website at
www.teaminternationalpublications.co.uk
and sign the booking form?

Or will you phone us now on: +44 (0)1286 660 330? It's a no-brainer!"

We hope this book will help you become highly successful
and a great achiever

About the Authors

Barry Thorogood - Team International

Barry founded Team International in 1990. Previous to that he was Senior Partner at Cornelyn International where in 1978 he pioneered Outdoor Management Development.

Before moving to Wales he was London Regional Manager with Rank Xerox. His sales team was 439% of target and he was elected to the Rank Xerox International Honours Club.

Prior to that he marketed the world's first colour copier; was a systems analyst in the City and a major accounts sales executive.

Preceding his corporate career, Barry was a qualified teacher and became a Deputy Head in a London school for maladjusted children; suitable qualifications for dealing with egocentric directors!

Barry has made several TV appearances and one programme in the series 'Leaders' was devoted entirely to his unique teaching methods. He has written and spoken extensively on Leadership, Teambuilding and Cultural Change. He has consistently worked with Main Boards of Directors with top UK companies.

He has an impressive track record of delivering successful change programmes. Barry is a highly skilled, experienced consultant with an endearing blend of visionary ideals mixed with a tough, down to earth realism. As a hard-up teacher, he regularly worked as a hod-carrier in the school holidays. He constantly challenges, is a seeker of the truth and is open and honest with a good sense of humour.

He acts as a process facilitator to Boards of Directors and is much in demand as a trusted and wise mentor. He instantly connects with all levels in a business and as such is a valuable conduit for difficult feedback.

Barry is an NLP practitioner, spent two years reading an MA in Management Learning at Lancaster, three years studying Infinite Tai Chi, three years learning Dru Yoga, is Reiki 1 qualified, a journey practitioner and an experienced group leader in Outdoor Activities.

He is a qualified RYA Coastal Skipper and his hobbies include climbing mountains, biking, sailing, surf canoeing, wind-surfing, swimming - he lives on the beach - football, para-gliding, yoga, tai-chi, dance, gardening, reading, films, music, charity work, mindfulness, meta-physics and meditation.

He is a devoted family man with two sons and four grandchildren.

He is also Consultant to Freshfields Animal Rescue, a charity that cares for and rehouses 1,500 animals every year, supported only by legacies and donations.

Barry rescued Ben, who is blind, and as you can see they go everywhere together.

Barry has a deep love of the Earth and of all living things.

As such he is a practising vegetarian, does not smoke, does not drink alcohol and is an engaged Buddhist (meditation + action!). He is a spiritual man and believes all paths lead to the same summit.

David Butler FCA MBE

"Remarkable" is the word that immediately springs to mind when describing David Butler.

David is a very fit triple amputee who found an unexploded bomb when 11 years old and lost both legs and a hand.

An extremely successful self-made businessman, his capabilities also extend to motor racing. David is pictured above with his beloved Left Hand Drive MGB.

He is the only disabled driver worldwide to have qualified for both an International Race and an International Rally Licence having competed in over 600 motorsport events, 110 races plus British and World Championship rallies.

He is Chairman of the British Motor Sport Association for the Disabled and sits with the Medical Panel of the governing body for motorsport in the UK representing all disabled drivers who wish to participate in motorsport. In 2010 he received an MBE for Services to Disabled Sport.

David is a Chartered Accountant but insists he still has a great sense of humour. He has worked in industry for over 30 years. It was his success in the sales sphere at Rank Xerox that made his name.

He spent 13 years at Rank Xerox, during which time he held the posts of Marketing Manager, National Sales Manager, Systems Business Division General Manager and finally the International Director of the Systems Business with a worldwide turnover in excess of $750 million and over 4,000 staff.

"Retiring" from the not so glamorous world travel, David developed an artificial intelligence software joint venture with Rank Xerox before setting up his own business consultancy.

David is still the youngest ever subject of the TV series "This is your Life" programme on which he appeared at the age of just 17.

Douglas Bader, the wartime legless fighter pilot ace, and David's hero, was the star guest.

David added narrative into a BBC TV film about the first disabled race driver - Archie Scott-Brown - while competing and crashing at Brands Hatch at one and the same time!

A conference speaker for Xerox and IBM, he has also taken part in numerous radio programmes about disability issues including:

 Woman's Hour
Start the Week,
Does He Take Sugar? and many others.

Pictured here with his grandson, he swims with a special flipper for up to three miles each week to keep fit.

David proudly carried the 2012 Olympic Torch through his home town of Hemel Hempstead where over 100,000 people turned out in the rain.

David also felt very privileged to be asked to drive the Orrery, the Solar system fire machine, in the 2012 Paralympic Opening Ceremony.

David is in the white shirt and brown bowler sitting on the front of the diesel engine monster machine.

He also did a choreographed dance routine (yes really, with best dancing legs on!) in a protest group in the middle of the stadium plus joining in the finale sing song - "I am what I am".

It was an unforgettable experience for him performing in front of the Royal Family and 80,000 people while trying not to run over or barbeque anyone.

Married for over 45 years (to the same lady!) David has two daughters, a grandson and a granddaughter.

Appendices

Please note all the documentation referred to in our book is available on our website in Word and PDF formats -

www.teaminternationalpublications.co.uk.

Working an exhibition

Tips should you find yourself working on a stand:

Be on time

Be very smart

Keep the stand tidy, tidy up AT ALL TIMES. Go round regularly

Keep the brochures topped up and neatly stacked

Do not consume food or drink on the stand

Do not hide behind displays - they are not "customer shelters". Get out there and "greet the people"

Have loads of business cards

Have your SPANCO system available - fill it in!

Collect prospects business cards like you collected things as a kid

Keep smiling!

Do not consume alcohol under any circumstances

Get to bed early - you have a long day ahead

Work in shifts. Organise rotas around the busy periods e.g. at the end of lectures or lunch.

Have your sales presentation with you - know how to sell from it and how to "sell off your brochures"

Have plenty of order forms available. You do not want to run out at the crucial moment! Top up your stock every day (or hour when busy)

If your product calls for demonstrations make sure you are perfect and very slick! There is nothing worse than a bungled demonstration. Have an engineer or technician on standby.

Know your way round the exhibition. Use the opportunity to gather information on your competitors and walk around the exhibition to get a "feel" for the market

If you have invited customers make sure you are there on time to meet them. Make sure you have some cash to buy them a drink or a sandwich.

Make it fun – remember the infectious nature of enthusiasm!

Telephone Selling Skills

Telephone Selling Script - Alternative dialogue tree

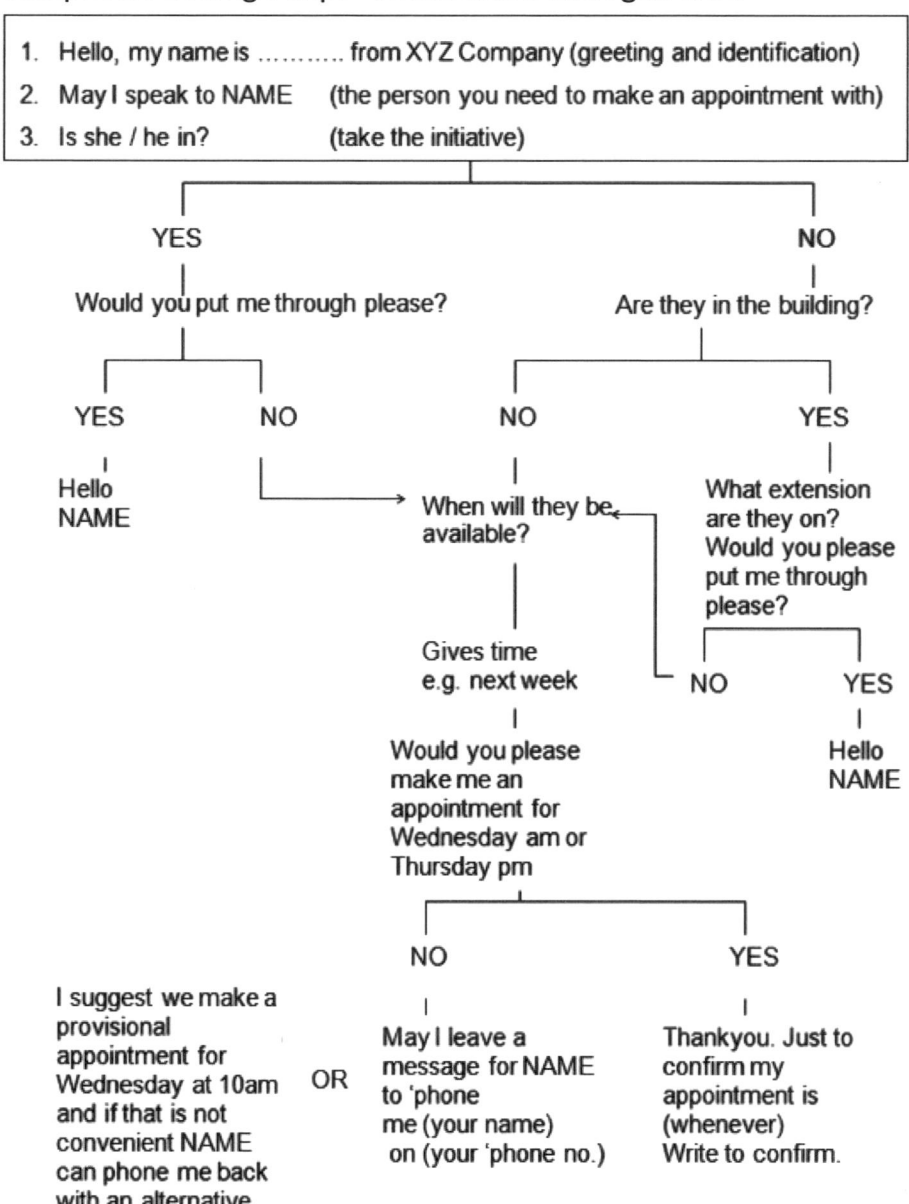

1. Hello, my name is .... from XYZ Company (greeting and identification)
2. May I speak to NAME   (the person you need to make an appointment with)
3. Is she / he in?   (take the initiative)

YES
|
Would you put me through please?

NO
|
Are they in the building?

YES
|
Hello
NAME

NO

NO
|
When will they be available?

YES
|
What extension are they on?
Would you please put me through please?

NO

YES
|
Hello
NAME

Gives time
e.g. next week
|
Would you please make me an appointment for Wednesday am or Thursday pm

NO
|
I suggest we make a provisional appointment for Wednesday at 10am and if that is not convenient NAME can phone me back with an alternative

OR

May I leave a message for NAME to 'phone me (your name) on (your 'phone no.)

YES
|
Thankyou. Just to confirm my appointment is (whenever) Write to confirm.

Sales Process Chart - Decision tree for a negative response.

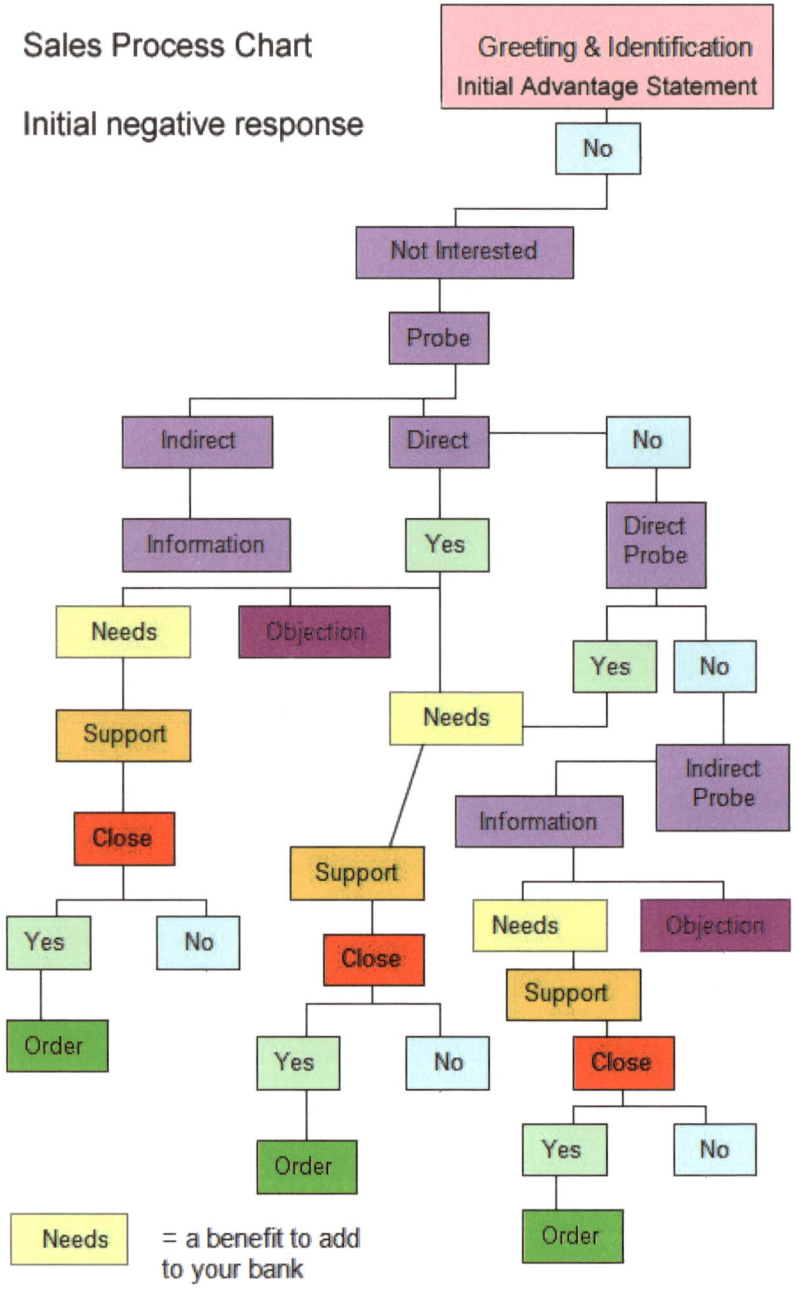

Sales Process Chart - Decision tree for objections and proof requirements.

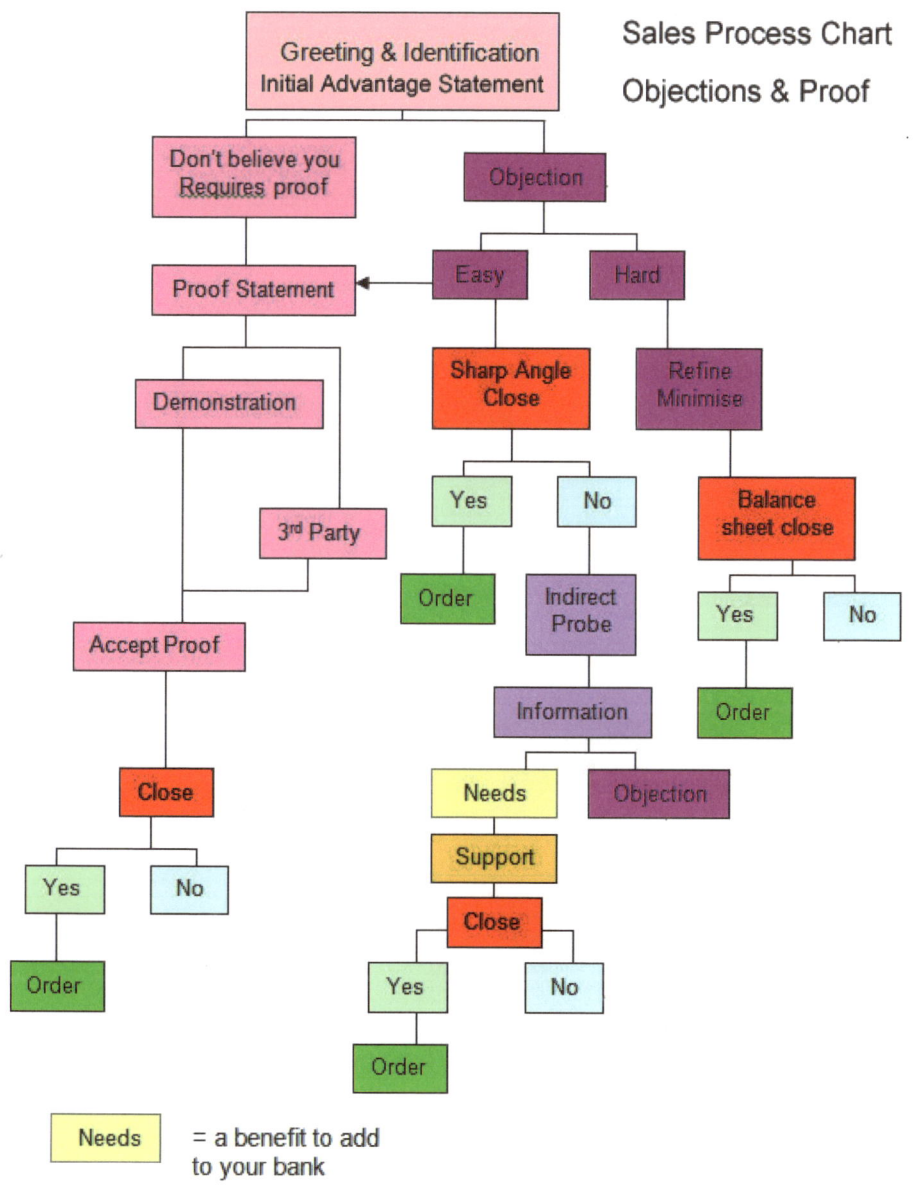

Sales Process Chart - Decision tree for a positive response.

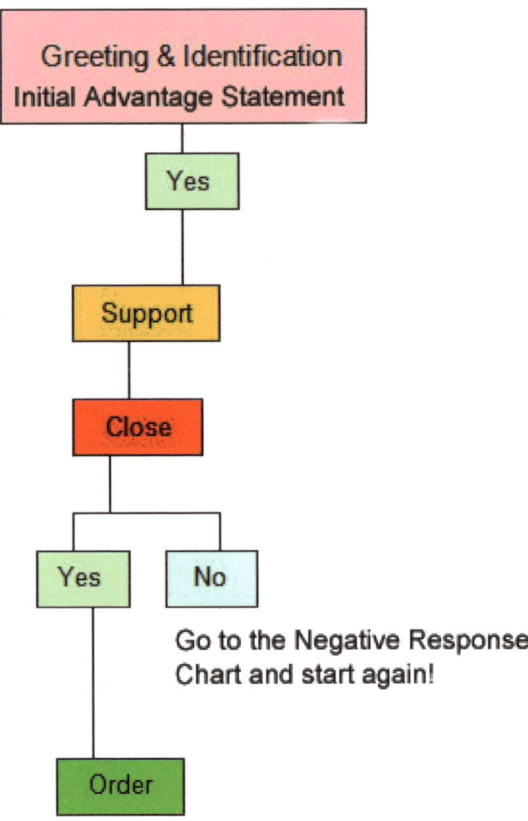

Sales Process Chart

A positive prospect

Greeting & Identification
Initial Advantage Statement

Yes

Support

Close

Yes   No

Go to the Negative Response
Chart and start again!

Order